Built to Last

By Joanne Mattern

ROURKE
PUBLISHING
www.rou

www.rourkepublishing.com

PHOTO CREDITS:
Front Cover: © Mirmoor; © Aginger, Back Cover: © halfshag; Title page © marema, beboy, Zacarias Pereira da Mata; Table of contents © Iafoto; Page 4/5 © Iafoto; Page 4 © Matt Trommer; Page 5 © RTimages, Darin Echelberger; Page 6/7 © marema; Page 7 © rob3000, Christopher Ewing; Page 8 © USGS; Page 9 © Alyssia Sheikh, beboy; Page 10/11 © Matt Trommer; Page 10 © Roypix; Page 11 © Igumnova Irina; Page 12/13 © FEMA; Page 12 © FEMA; Page 14/15 © Jerry Sharp; Page 15 © Kuttelvaserova, Stephen Finn; Page 16/17 © Gina Sanders; Page 17 © donross; Page 18 © Zacarias Pereira da Mata, Alyssia Sheikh; Page 19 © aarrows, U.S. Navy photo by Mass Communication Specialist 3rd Class Alexander Tidd; Page 20 © Nick Tzolov; Page 21 © NOAA; Page 22 © noaa; Page 23 © noaa; Page 24/25 © RTimages; Page 24 © Alyssia Sheikh; Page 26 © Gregor K ervina, Alyssia Sheikh; Page 27 © Iafoto, NOAA; Page 28/29 © iBird; Page 29 © Anthro; Page 30 © iBird, USGS ; Page 31 © NOAA, R. Cherubin, Alyssia Sheikh; Page 33 © Christopher Tan Teck Hean, Alyssia Sheikh; Page 34 © Peter J. Wilson; Page 35 © Jim Parkin; Page 36/37 © Brian Weed; Page 36 © NASA; Page 38 © NOAA; Page 39 © Andy Z.; Page 40 © Alyssia Sheikh; Page 41 © Lisa F. Young, karamysh; Page 42 © arindambanerjee; Page 43 © Brad Wilkins, Path2k6; Page 44 © Leonard G.; Page 45 © David Hughes, Bill Bradley

Edited by Precious McKenzie

Cover design by Teri Intzegian
Layout: Blue Door Publishing, FL

Library of Congress Cataloging-in-Publication Data

Mattern, Joanne
  Built To Last / Joanne Mattern
  p. cm. -- (Let's Explore Science)
  ISBN 978-1-61741-787-0 (hard cover) (alk. paper)
  ISBN 978-1-61741-989-8 (soft cover)
Library of Congress Control Number: 2011924832

Rourke Publishing
Printed in the United States of America, North Mankato, Minnesota
060711
060711CL

www.rourkepublishing.com - rourke@rourkepublishing.com
Post Office Box 643328 Vero Beach, Florida 32964

Table of Contents

CHAPTER ONE

What Are Nature's Forces?

Nature is usually calm and quiet. Most people on Earth go about their days feeling safe and secure. However, nature sometimes gets out of control. Sometimes nature's forces unleash destruction on the planet we call home. The forces that destroy are the same ones that formed our planet and affect our lives.

Earth is made of several layers. The surface of the Earth is called the **crust**. Although the Earth's surface looks thick and strong, it is really quite thin. The thickest part of the Earth's crust is only about 60 miles (97 kilometers) thick.

The **mantle** lies under the surface. The mantle is a layer of molten, or melted, rock. The **core** is at the center of the Earth. The core is made of metal and is about 44,000 miles (70,811 kilometers) in diameter.

The Earth's crust is thinnest under the oceans. The crust there is only 4 to 7 miles (6.4 - 11.3 kilometers) thick. The Earth's crust is thickest under the continents.

Mantle

Core

Crust

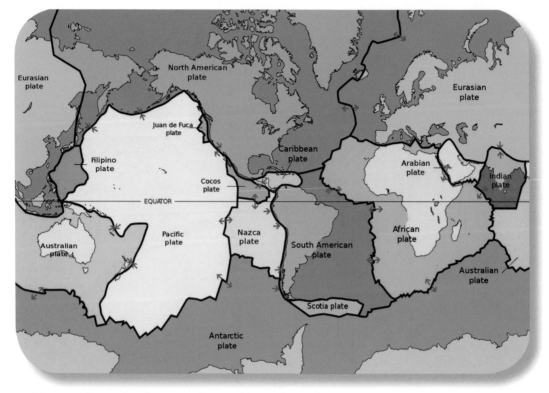

This map shows the plates on the Earth's surface. These plates are in constant motion. The edges of these plates, known as plate boundaries, are where geological events such as earthquakes occur. Plate boundaries are also where Earth's features such as mountains, volcanoes, ocean ridges and trenches are created.

The land under your feet may seem solid, but it is actually moving all the time. This movement occurs because the Earth's crust and the outer layer of the mantle rest on flat pieces called **tectonic plates**. The plates move around on top of the mantle. Usually this movement is gentle. However, plates slide and bang against each other, causing earthquakes.

Sometimes hot molten rocks inside the Earth escape through a crack in the surface. These cracks are called volcanoes. The hot molten rock, or lava, that flows from a volcano can destroy buildings.

RING OF FIRE

Asia

United States of America

South America

Australia

9

The weather around us can also turn violent at any time. Weather occurs in the Earth's **atmosphere**. The air above the Earth is always moving. When the air moves quickly, powerful winds can damage the Earth.

Precipitation is another part of the weather. Precipitation can be in the form of rain, snow, hail, or sleet. Precipitation provides water to Earth. However, heavy rainstorms can cause flooding, and heavy snowstorms can damage property.

Did You Know?

When hurricanes approach low-lying coastal areas residents are advised to evacuate to strong buildings that are inland and on higher ground. Hurricane shelters are buildings that are used for something else, such as this football stadium in New Orleans, Louisiana. When Hurricane Katrina hit it became a shelter for many residents.

Nature's forces come in many forms. However, people have learned to adapt to these forces and create buildings and other structures that can withstand disasters. These strong structures allow people to live through disasters.

CHAPTER TWO

The Power of Water

Water is one of nature's most powerful forces. Usually, water is helpful because all living things need water. The power of water's movement is also used to create energy and run machines.

As with all of nature's forces, water can get out of control and cause damage. When water gets out of control, the result is a flood. A flood occurs when water covers an area that is usually dry.

Most floods happen naturally. A bad storm can pour several inches of rain on an area. The rain causes rivers and streams to overflow. The result is flooding.

DANGER FLASH FLOODS

Did You Know?

Sometimes people have a warning that a flood is coming. Other floods, called flash floods, strike so quickly that there is no time to warn people to get out of the way.

Building Smart

This levee is a man-made embankment raised to prevent a river from overflowing. The Mississippi River levee system extends over 3,500 miles (5,600 kilometers).

A flood can cover roads and rush through buildings, causing a lot of damage. The force of moving water is also very dangerous. A flood can move objects inside a house, wash cars out of a parking lot, and even sweep a building off its foundation.

Building Smart

Stilt houses are built in coastal areas and other flood zones. By raising homes 10 to 12 feet (3.5 – 4 meters) from the ground homes are protected during floods and high winds.

Destructive floods can also come from the movement of the ocean's waves. A **tsunami** is a series of giant ocean waves. Tsunamis are most common in the Pacific Ocean. They often occur after earthquakes or volcanic eruptions.

Tsunamis are deadly because they move so fast. A tsunami wave moves up to 600 miles (965 kilometers) an hour. As the speeding waves reach shallow water near land, it causes the water to pile up in a huge wave that can be up to 100 feet (30 meters) high. When this wave reaches land, it floods everything in its path.

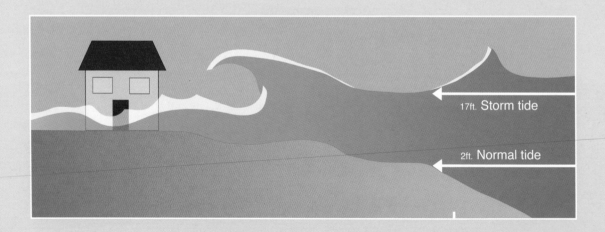

17ft. Storm tide

2ft. Normal tide

Did You Know?

In March 2011, a powerful earthquake struck northern Japan. The quake triggered a tsunami that wiped out large areas of the coast and killed thousands of people. The waves from the tsunami spread all the way across the ocean to the coasts of California and Oregon.

JAPAN

CHAPTER THREE

Rushing Winds

Wind can also be a powerful force. The wind is an essential part of weather because it moves weather systems from one area to another. This movement of air is the wind.

Like water, wind can be used to create energy and power machines. However, too much wind can cause destruction. High winds can knock over trees, blow roofs off houses, and bring down power lines.

Building Smart

Hurricane shutters can be found on homes in coastal areas and other hurricane prone areas. These shutters protect windows and doors. They protect against wind and debris.

LARGE STORM CLOUDS

LOWEST PRESSURE

Satellite photos help us get clear views of a hurricane's eye. The eye, or center, of a hurricane is the point of calm. Winds and rains die down when the eye of the storm passes over land. But watch out, because when the eye moves away, the storm begins all over again.

Hurricanes are powerful storms that combine wind and water. A hurricane is an area of low **air pressure** that forms over the ocean. Storm clouds whirl around the area of low pressure creating powerful winds and heavy rains. Winds over 80 miles (129 kilometers) per hour create huge waves in the ocean and more damage on land.

During these storms, an area of low air pressure causes the surface of the ocean to rise. When a hurricane passes over coastal land, the rising water can rush over the land, causing a **storm surge**— a flood— that can stretch for miles.

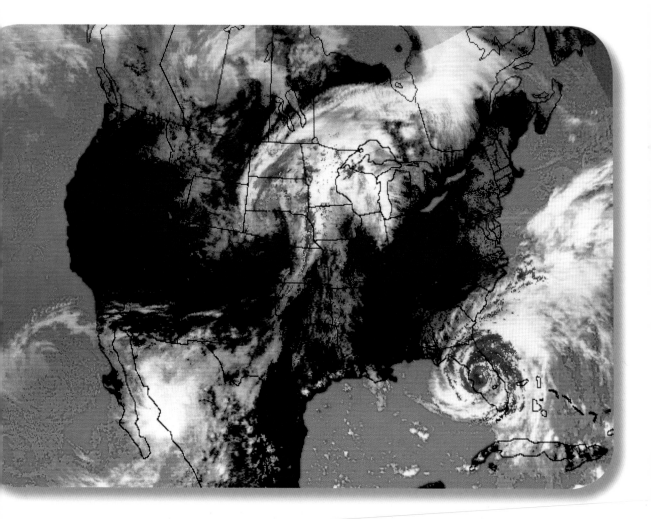

Weather crews track a hurricane closely because just one hurricane can affect the flood levels and wind speeds for hundreds of miles.

Did You Know?

"Hurricane" is the name of a tropical storm that occurs in the North Atlantic Ocean, the Caribbean Sea, the Gulf of Mexico, and the Northeast Pacific Ocean. The same type of storm is called a typhoon in the Northwest Pacific Ocean. In the Indian Ocean and the waters around Australia, these storms are called cyclones.

Meteorologists use computer programs that calculate water temperature, air pressure, and wind speed to determine a hurricane's path.

Planes used to track hurricanes are called Hurricane Hunters.

23

Frozen water can be a powerful force as well. When temperatures are below freezing (32°F, 0°C), precipitation usually falls as snow instead of rain. Heavy snow can block roads and make it dangerous to drive or walk. Many people have gotten lost and even frozen to death in snowstorms.

SNOWMELT SYSTEM

2 The heated water travels through tubing laid underneath the pavement and sidewalks, melting the snow and ice.

3 The system can melt approximately 1 inch of snow per hour at 15-20 degrees F (-9--6 degrees C). Windy conditions may slow the process.

1 Waste heat is generated at the power plant and discharged to the snowmelt system.

4 After the water cools it is discharged into Lake Macatawa.

LAKE WATER

Shoveling snow from sidewalks may become a thing of the past as more and more people are installing heating systems in the sidewalks, driveways, and parking lots around their homes and businesses. Some of the heaters use geothermal energy, or energy that comes from within the Earth. The heaters can't be seen because the are installed under the concrete or pavement.

Ice is another dangerous force of nature that can damage property and cause death and injury.

Wind and snow can also combine in a powerful storm called a blizzard. A blizzard is a storm that combines heavy snowfall with winds of more than 35 miles (56 kilometers) per hour. These strong winds blow the snow around so it is impossible to see.

Winds are a big part of nature's most powerful storm, the tornado. Tornadoes are small areas of spinning winds. Torna occur when two air masses collide and swirl around, creatir powerful winds that can destroy everything in their path. Tornadoes are usually small storms that last only a few minu Tornadoes can form anywhere, but the central part of the U States has more tornadoes than any other part of the world

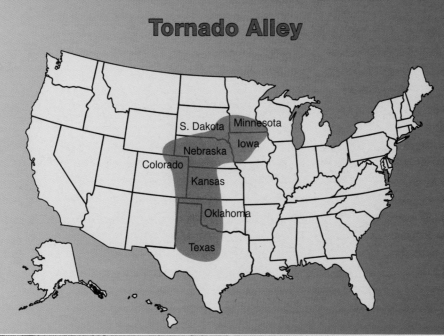

Tornado Alley

S. Dakota Minnesota

Iowa

Nebraska

Colorado

Kansas

Oklahoma

Texas

The states in Tornado Alley have recorded more F5 category tornadoes than anywhere else. Residents need to always be prepared.

id You Know?

ornado's path can be so
row that it will destroy
ouse and leave the house
t door unharmed.

Building Smart

People that live in tornado prone areas may have basements or cellars to take shelter in during a storm. In homes without a basement a windowless room can be used as a shelter from a storm.

CHAPTER FOUR

Moving Earth

Wind and water are just two examples of nature's powerful forces. The Earth itself can also be a powerful force. When the Earth moves, the whole face of the planet can change.

Earthquakes happen along the edges of Earth's tectonic plates. The area where two plates meet is called a fault. Large pieces of rock push and rub against each other along a fault. In time, one of the rocks might break. When this happens, it causes a type of energy called **seismic waves**. Seismic waves travel through the ground, causing it to shake.

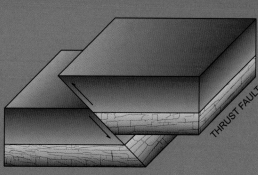

THRUST FAULT

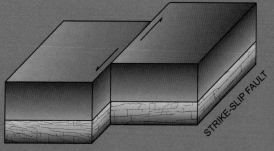

STRIKE-SLIP FAULT

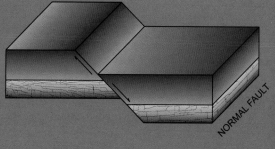

NORMAL FAULT

Shifting fault lines thrust the Earth and create new land formations.

Earthquakes happen all the time, but most are so small people barely notice them. However, bad things can happen in a large earthquake. The movement of the Earth can cause buildings and roads to collapse.

Charles Richter

Did You Know?

Earthquakes are measured on a scale invented by Charles Richter. The strongest earthquake ever recorded occurred in Chile in 1960. It measured 9.5 on the Richter scale.

Did You Know?

A powerful earthquake struck Alaska in 1964, causing many landslides. The shape of the coastline in the towns of Seward and Valdez was permanently changed.

Building Smart

Many high-rise buildings in earthquake prone areas are built on rollers. When an earthquake occurs the rollers move and the building stays in place.

The Earth can move for other reasons besides earthquakes. Landslides and mudslides are dangerous and deadly events where the ground actually slides away. These disasters often happen during or after a heavy rain. The ground becomes so **saturated** with water it cannot hold together. Water runs down a hill, creating a wall of dirt, mud, and rocks racing down the hill and slamming into the ground below.

Scientists have discovered that split level houses built with retaining walls in and around them withstand the forces of landslides better than traditional houses. These houses built into the sides of mountains and hills look like giant steps.

When building in landslide prone areas, builders clear only the land they need for the house and keep the rest of the plants in place.

CHAPTER FIVE

FIRE!

Fire is another one of nature's most powerful forces. One of the most dangerous types of fire is a wildfire. A wildfire usually starts in the forest or in brushy areas. These fires can become very large and impossible to control. They can rage for days or even weeks, destroying everything in their path.

While some wildfires are caused by lightning strikes, most wildfires are caused by people. A person can start a fire by dropping a lit cigarette onto dry leaves or brush on the ground. Another common cause is a campfire that is not completely extinguished when the campers leave.

Did You Know?

Wildfires aren't all bad. Some pine trees need the heat of a fire to open their cones and spread seeds that grow into new trees. Wildfires can also clear an area of dead leaves, **underbrush**, and trees.

Sometimes forest rangers start controlled burns. Controlled burns are a way for rangers to clear away underbrush before a larger, uncontrolled wildfire can begin. It is a way to manage the wilderness and keep people safe.

The largest wildfire in California started in the Cleveland National Forest in 2003. Three days later, the fire spread to the towns of Cuyamaca and Julien, about 40 miles (64.4 kilometers) east of San Diego. More than 2,200 houses were destroyed and 14 people were killed in the blaze.

Did You Know?

Fires can destroy major cities too. In 1666, the Great Fire of London started in a small bakeshop. The fire spread quickly through the city's crowded wooden houses and destroyed 80 percent of the city.

Hot, dry winds can make wildfires worse. Winds called Santa
Anas often strike southern California. These winds move from the
east, pushing hot, dry air from the western deserts to the California
coast. Santa Ana winds can make a small wildfire big. Combining
nature's forces often leads to even more disaster.

Santa Ana Winds

Satellites help us locate the patterns of dangerous winds.

Building Smart

Some buildings have built-in sprinkler systems. When a fire is detected in the building the sprinkler system is automatically set off, dousing the fire with water.

CHAPTER SIX

Preparing For Disaster

Meteorologists are scientists who study the weather. Meteorologists use computer models, **radar**, and other technology to study weather patterns and make predictions about upcoming storms. These tools help meteorologists figure out when and where a storm might strike and how severe it will be. This information can be used to warn people to **evacuate** or take steps to protect their homes and property.

Technology, such as the mobile doppler, gathers data on storm systems and sends warnings to people.

Engineers work to prevent and control flooding. Engineers design dams and levees in an effort to control and even change the flow of water. These efforts can help control raging rivers or ocean waves.

Scientists called **seismologists** study earthquakes. They track and measure tremors and other movements of the Earth and use that data to predict when a major earthquake might occur.

Technology can keep people safe from nature's forces in other ways. Countries in the Pacific and Indian Oceans have tsunami warning systems. These systems use machines to sense waves and other movements in the ocean. If a tsunami is predicted, governments will issue warnings so people will have time to evacuate to safety.

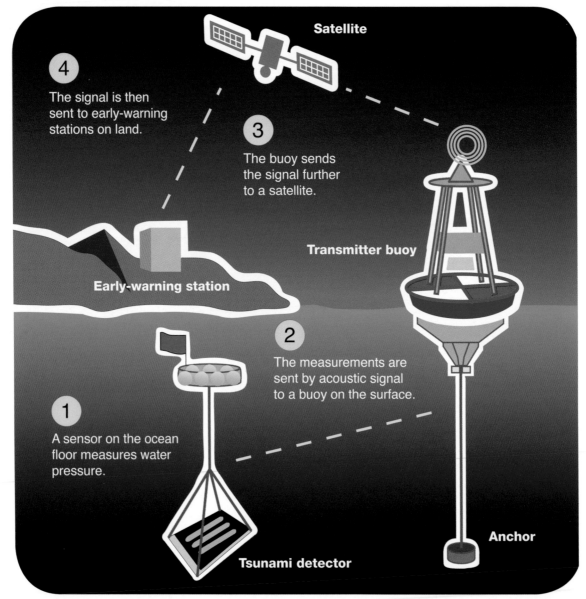

Satellite

4 The signal is then sent to early-warning stations on land.

3 The buoy sends the signal further to a satellite.

Transmitter buoy

Early-warning station

2 The measurements are sent by acoustic signal to a buoy on the surface.

1 A sensor on the ocean floor measures water pressure.

Anchor

Tsunami detector

Despite the best efforts of meteorologists, scientists, and engineers, disasters do happen. During and after a disaster, emergency agencies, such as the Red Cross, work to find shelter, medical care, and supplies for people who have lost their homes and belongings.

41

CHAPTER SEVEN

Building Smart

Buildings and other structures can provide safe shelter during a disaster. That's why it's so important that they be built to withstand nature's forces. Engineers and builders have learned how to build houses, businesses, and bridges that can withstand nature's forces.

Did You Know?

In January 2010, a powerful earthquake struck Haiti and killed more than 300,000 people. In February, an even more powerful earthquake struck Chile, but only about 560 people were killed. One reason fewer people died in Chile was that the homes there did not collapse in the earthquake.

Earthquakes are one of nature's most destructive forces. During a severe earthquake, thousands of people can be killed. Many of those deaths occur when buildings collapse on the people inside.

X-bracing with steel is one technique engineers use to help a structure remain upright and intact during an earthquake.

One of the most important ways to make a building safe is to build it in the right place. Some soil is soft and loose. When an earthquake strikes and the Earth moves, that soft soil cannot hold up the building on top of it.

It's important that the building itself be able to stand up to an earthquake. Most earthquake-safe buildings include **tiedown systems**. These systems use steel rods and straps to anchor the building to the ground. Steel bends instead of breaking, so steel rods help the building stay in one piece during a quake. An earthquake-proof building might sway or rock during an earthquake, but it won't fall down!

The John Hancock Center, in Chicago, has external x-bracing.

43

Civil engineers design bridges that will bend or sway during an earthquake but reinforcements will not let the bridge collapse.

Bridges also need to be designed to withstand quakes. Engineers can add many features to make a bridge earthquake-safe. Bearings absorb side to side vibrations and protect the deck from breaking apart. Steel bars are used to support the bridge and help it bend instead of snapping apart.

Rain and wind can also do a lot of damage to a building. The force of wind can push against the roof and blow the roof right off

the building. To prevent this, many buildings in areas that get hurricanes are built with braces that hold the roof to the walls of the building. Hurricane straps or clips can also be used to attach the roof to the walls.

Rainwater can also damage a building. The best way to keep rainwater out of a house is to direct it away from the structure. Gutters carry rain from the roof and move it away from the house. People can also build their house on higher ground. This process forces water to flow away from the building.

By building strong structures and finding ways to deal with natural disasters, we can all try to live safely on Earth.

Glossary

air pressure (AIR PRESH-ur): the weight of air pressing down on Earth's surface

atmosphere (AT-muhss-fihr): the layer of gases surrounding Earth

core (KOR): the center part of Earth's interior

crust (KRUHST): the solid outer layer of Earth

engineers (en-juh-NIHRZ): people who are trained to design and build machines or structures

evacuate (i-VAK-yoo-ate): to leave an area because of an emergency

hurricanes (HUR-uh-kanez): tropical storms in the Atlantic Ocean, Caribbean Sea, and the Gulf of Mexico that produce high winds and heavy rains

mantle (MAN-tuhl): the layer of rock between Earth's crust and core

meteorologists (mee-tee-ur-OL-oh-jists): scientists who study the weather

precipitation (pri-sip-i-TAY-shuhn): moisture that falls from clouds, including rain, snow, or hail

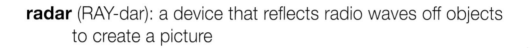

radar (RAY-dar): a device that reflects radio waves off objects to create a picture

satellite (SAT-uh-lite): a spacecraft that orbits the Earth and sends back photos or other information

saturated (SACH-uh-ray-ted): filled with water

seismic waves (SIZE-mik WAYVZ): vibrations that travel through Earth

seismologists (size-MOHL-uh-jists): scientists who study earthquakes

storm surge (STORM SURJ): rush of water over the land caused by low air pressure over the ocean

tectonic plates (tek-TON-ik PLAYTS): rigid pieces that make up Earth's surface

tiedown systems (TYE-down siss-TUHMZ): a method of building that uses steel straps and rods to anchor a building to the ground

tsunami (tsoo-NAH-mee): a series of powerful ocean waves, usually caused by an earthquake or volcanic eruption

underbrush (UHN-dur-bruhsh): shrubs or bushes that grow beneath taller trees

Index

Websites to Visit

www.eduweb.com/portfolio/bridgetoclassroom/engineeringfor.html

www.popularmechanics.com/science/environment/natural-disasters/4324941

www.yourdiscovery.com/earth/

www.fema.gov/kids/index.htm

www.chicagohs.org/history/fire.html

www.stonebreakerbuilders.com/news/
how-the-forces-of-nature-affect-your-home/

www.usatoday.com/weather/wsanta.html

http://bereadyescambia.com/pdf/windbrochure.pdf

About the Author

Joanne Mattern has written hundreds of nonfiction books for children. Nature, science, and natural disasters are some of her favorite topics, so BUILT TO LAST was a very interesting book for her to write! Joanne grew up on the banks of the Hudson River in New York State and still lives in the area with her husband, four children, and many pets.